Book 1
Windows 8 Tips for Beginners

BY SAM KEY

&

Book 2
HTML Professional Programming Made Easy

BY SAM KEY

Book 1
Windows 8 Tips for Beginners

BY SAM KEY

A Simple, Easy, and Efficient Guide to a Complex System of Windows 8!

Programming Box Set #96: Windows 8 Tips for Beginners & HTML Professional Programming Made Easy

Programming Box Set #96: Windows 8 Tips for Beginners & HTML Professional Programming Made Easy

Table Of Contents

Introduction

I want to thank you and congratulate you for purchasing the book, "Windows 8 Tips for Beginners: A Simple, easy, and efficient guide to a complex system of windows 8!"

This book contains proven steps and strategies on how to familiarize yourself with the new features of Windows 8 which were designed to make your computing experience simpler and more enjoyable. You will not only learn how to navigate through Windows 8 , but you will also learn how Windows 8 is similar to and different from the older versions so you can easily adjust and take advantage of the benefits that Windows 8 has in store for you.

Thanks again for purchasing this book, I hope you enjoy it!

Chapter 1: How is Windows 8 Different from Previous Versions?

With Windows 8, Microsoft launched a lot of new changes and features, some of which are minor , but others are major. Some of the changes you can see in Windows 8 are the redesigned interface, enhanced security and other online features.

Changes in the Interface

The most glaring change you will observe when you first open your computer with Windows 8 is that the screen looks completely different from older Windows versions. The Windows 8 interface has new features such as Start screen, hot corners, and live tiles.

- The Start screen will be the main screen where you will find all of your installed programs and they will be in the form of "tiles". You can personalize your Start Screen by rearranging the tiles, selecting a background image and changing the color scheme.

- You can navigate through Windows 8 using the "hot corners", which you activate by hovering the mouse pointer over the corners of the screen. For instance, if you want to switch to another open application, hover your mouse in the top-left corner of your screen and then click on the app.

- Certain apps have Live Tile functions, which enable you to see information even if the app itself is not open. For instance, you can easily see the current weather on the Weather app tile from your Start screen; if you want to see more information, you can just click on the app to open it.

- You can now find many of the settings of your computer in the Charms bar that you can open by hovering the mouse in the bottom-right or top-right corner of your computer screen.

Online Features in Windows 8

Because of the ease of accessing Internet now, many people have started to save their documents and other data online. Microsoft has made it easier to save on the cloud through their OneDrive service (this was formerly called SkyDrive). Windows 8 is capable of linking to OneDrive and other online social networks such as Twitter and Facebook in a seamless manner.

To connect your computer to OneDrive, sign in using your free Microsoft account instead of your own computer account. When you do this, all of the contacts, files and other information stored in your OneDrive are all in your Start screen. You can also use another computer to sign in to your Microsoft account and access all of your OneDrive files. You can also easily link your Flickr, Twitter and Facebook accounts to Windows 8 so you will be able to see the updates straight from your Start screen. You can also do this through the People app which is included in Windows 8.

Other Features

- The Desktop is now simpler for enhanced speed. Yes, the Desktop is still included in Windows 8 and you can still manage your documents or open your installed programs through the Desktop. However, with Windows 8, a number of the transparency effects that frequently caused Windows Vista and Windows 7 to slow down are now gone. This allows the Desktop to operate smoother on nearly all computers.

- The Start menu, once considered as a vital feature in previous Windows versions, is now the Start screen. You can now open your installed programs or search for your files through the Start screen. This can be quite disorienting if you are just starting with Windows 8.

- Windows 8 has enhanced security because of its integrated antivirus program referred to as Windows Defender. This antivirus program is also useful in protecting you from different kinds of malware. In addition, it can aid in keeping you and your computer secure by telling you which data each of your installed apps can access. For instance, certain apps can access your location, so if you do not want other people to know where you are, just change your preference in the settings/configuration part of your apps.

How to Use Windows 8

Because Windows 8 is not like the older versions, it will possibly change how you have been using your computer. You may need quite some time to get accustomed to the new features, but you just need to remember that those changes are necessary to enhance your computing experience. For instance, if you have used older Windows versions, you may be used to clicking on the Start button to launch programs. You need to get used to using the Start screen with Windows 8. Of course, you can still use the Desktop view to make file and folder organization easier and to launch older programs.

You may need to switch between the Desktop view and the Start screen to work on your computer. Don't feel bad if you feel disoriented at first because you will get used to it. Moreover, if you just use your computer to surf the internet, you may be spending majority of your time in the Start screen anyway.

Chapter 2: How to Get Started with Windows 8

Windows 8 can truly be bewildering at the start because of the many changes done to the interface. You will need to learn effective navigation of both the Start screen and Desktop view. Even though the Desktop view appears similar to the older Windows versions, it has one major change that you need to get used to – the Start menu is no more.

In this chapter, you will learn how to work with the apps and effectively navigate Windows 8 using the Charms bar. You will learn where to look for the features that you could previously find in the Start menu.

How to Sign In

While setting up Windows 8, you will be required to create your own account name and password that you will use to sign in. You can also opt to create other account names and associate each account name with a specific Microsoft account. You will then see your own user account name and photo (if you have uploaded one). Key in your password and press enter. To select another user, click on the back arrow to choose from the available options. After you have signed in, the Start screen will be displayed.

How to Navigate Windows 8

You can use the following ways to navigate your way through Windows 8

• You can use the hot corners to navigate through Windows 8. You can use them whether you are in the Desktop view or in the Start screen. Simply hover your mouse in the corner of the screen to access the hot corners. You will see a tile or a toolbar that you can then click to open. All the corners perform various tasks. For instance, hovering the pointer on the lower-left corner will return you to the Start screen. The upper-left corner will allow you to switch to the last application that you were using. The lower-right or upper-right corners gives you access to the Charms bar where you can either manage your printers or adjust the settings of your computer. Hover your mouse towards the upper-left corner and then move your mouse down to see the list of the different applications that you are simultaneously using. You can simply on any application to go back to it.

- You can also navigate through Windows 8 through different keyboard shortcuts.
    - Alt+Tab is the most useful shortcut; you use it to switch between open applications in both the Start screen and Desktop view.
    - You can use the Windows key to go back to the Start screen. It also works in both the Desktop view and Start screen.
    - From the Start screen, you can go to the Desktop view by clicking on Windows+D.
- You can access the settings and other features of your computer through the toolbar referred to as Charms bar. Place your mouse pointer on the bottom-right or top-right corner of your screen to display the Charms bar wherein you can see the following icons or "charms":
    - The Search charm allows you to look for files, apps or settings on your computer. However, a simpler method to do a search is through the Start screen wherein you can simply key in the name of the application or file that you want to find.
    - You can think of the Share charm as a "copy and paste" attribute that is included in Windows 8 to make it easier for you to work with your computer. Using the Share charm, you can "copy" data like a web address or a picture from one app and then "paste" it onto another application. For instance, if you are reading a certain article in the Internet, you can share the website address in your Mail application so you can send it to a friend.
    - The Start charm will allow you to go back to the Start screen. If you are currently on the Start screen, the Start charm will launch the latest app that you used.

- The Devices charm displays all of the hardware devices that are linked to your computer such as monitors and printers.

- Through the Settings charm, you can open both the general setting of your computer and the settings of the application that you are presently using. For instance, if you are presently using the web browser, you can access the Internet Options through the Settings charm.

How to Work with the Start Screen Applications

You may need to familiarize yourself with the Start screen applications because they are quite different from the "classic" Windows applications from previous versions. The apps in Windows 8 fill the whole screen rather than launching in a window. However, you can still do multi-tasking by launching two or more applications next to each other.

- To open an application from the Start screen, look for the app that you want to launch and click on it.

- To close an application hover your mouse at the top portion of the application, and you will notice that the cursor will become a hand icon, click and hold your mouse and then drag it towards the bottommost part of the screen and then release. When the app has closed, you will go back to the Start screen.

How to View Apps Side by Side

Even though the applications normally fill up the whole screen, Windows 8 still allows you to snap an application to the right or left side and then launch other applications beside it. For instance, you can work on a word document while viewing the calendar app. Here are the steps to view applications side by side:

1. Go to the Start screen and then click on the first app that you want to open.

2. Once the app is open, click on the title bar and drag the window to the left or right side of your computer screen.

3. Release your mouse and you will see that the application has snapped to the side of your computer screen.

4. You can go back to the Start screen by clicking at any empty space of the computer screen.

5. Click on another application that you want to open.

6. You will now see the applications displayed side by side. You can also adjust the size of the applications by dragging the bar.

Please note that the snapping feature is intended to work with a widescreen monitor. Your minimum screen resolution should be 1366 x 768 pixels to enjoy the snapping feature fully. If your monitor has a bigger screen, you will be able to snap more than two apps simultaneously.

How to cope with the Start menu

Many people have already complained about the missing Start menu in Windows 8. For many Windows users, the Start menu is a very vital feature because they use to open applications, look for files, launch the Control Panel and shut down their computer. You can actually do all of these things in Windows 8 too, but you will now have to look for them in different locations.

- There are a number of ways to launch an application in Windows 8. You can launch an app by clicking the application icon on the taskbar or double-clicking the application shortcut form the Desktop view or clicking the application tile in the Start screen.

- You can look for an app or a file by pressing the Windows key to go back to the Start screen. When you are there, you can simply key in the filename or app name that you want to look for. The results of your search will be immediately displayed underneath the search bar. You will also see a list of recommended web searches underneath the search results.

- You can launch the Control Panel by going to the Desktop view and then hovering your mouse in the lower-right corner of the computer screen to display the Charms bar and then selecting Settings. From the Settings Pane, look for and choose Control Panel.

After the Control Panel pops up, you can start choosing your preferred settings.

- You can shut down your computer by hovering the mouse in the lower-right corner of your screen to display the Charms bar and then selecting Settings. Click on the Power icon and then choose Shut Down.

Start Screen Options

If you prefer to continue working with the Desktop view more often, you actually have a number of alternatives that can let your computer operate more like the older Windows versions. One of these alternatives is the "boot your computer directly to the Desktop" rather than the Start screen. Here are the steps to change your Start screen options:

1. Return to the Desktop view.

2. Right-click the taskbar then choose Properties.

3. You will then see a dialog box where you can choose the options that you want to change.

Chapter 3: How to Personalize Your Start Screen

If you are open to the idea of spending most of your time on the Start screen of your computer, there are different ways you can do to personalize it based on your preferences. You can change the background color and image, rearrange the applications, pin applications and create application groups.

- You can change the background of your Start screen by hovering the mouse in the lower-right corner of your screen to open up the Charms bar and then selecting the Settings icon. Choose Personalize and then choose your preferred color scheme and background image.

- You can change the lock screen picture by displaying the Charms bar again and the selecting the Settings icon. Choose Change PC settings and then choose Lock screen that is located near to the topmost part of the screen. Choose your preferred image from the thumbnail photos shown. You can also opt to click on Browse to choose your own photos. You will see the lock screen every time you return to your computer after leaving it inactive for a set number of minutes. However, you can also manually lock your screen by clicking on your account name and then choosing Lock.

- You can change your own account photo by displaying the Charms bar and then choosing the Settings icon. Click on the Change PC setting and choose Account picture. You can look for your own photos by clicking Browse, will let you browse the folders in your computer. Once you find the picture you want to use, click on Choose image to set it as your account picture. If you are running a laptop, you can also use the built-in webcam to take a picture of yourself for your account photo.

How to Customize the Start Screen Applications

You do not really need to put up with the pre-arranged apps on your Start screen. You can change how they look by rearranging them based on your own preference. You can move an app by clicking, holding and dragging the application to your preferred location. Let go of your mouse and the app tile will automatically move to the new place.

You may also think that the animation in the live tiles is very disturbing while you are working. Do not worry because you can simply turn the animation off so that you will only see a plain background. You can do this by right-clicking the application that you wish to change. A toolbar pop up from the bottom part of your computer screen. Simply choose Turn live tile off and the animation if you don't want real-time notifications.

How to Pin Applications to the Start Screen

By default, you won't be able to see all of the installed applications on the Start screen. However, you can easily "pin" your favorite apps on the Start screen so you can access them easily. You can do this by clicking the arrow found in the bottom-left corner of your Start screen. You will then see the list of all the applications that you have installed. Look for the app you want to pin and the right-click it. You will see Pin to Start at the lowest part of the screen. Click on it to pin your app.

To unpin or remove an application from the Start screen, right-click the app icon you want to remove and then choose "Unpin from Start".

How to Create Application Groups

There are more ways to bring organization to your apps. One way is to create an app group wherein you can similar apps together. You can give a specific name for each app group for easier retrieval. You can create a new application group by clicking, holding and dragging an application to the right side until you see it on an empty space of the Start screen. Let go of your mouse to let the app be inside its own application group. You will be able to see a distinct space between the new app group that you have just created and the other app groups. You can then drag other apps into the new group.

You can name your new application group by right clicking any of the apps on the Start screen and then clicking Name group at the top of the application group. When choosing a group name, opt for shorter, but more descriptive names. After you have keyed in your group name, press the Enter key.

Chapter 4: How to Manage Your Files and Folders

The File Explorer found in the Desktop view is very handy in managing files and folders in your computer. If you are familiar with older Windows version, File Explorer is actually the same as Windows Explorer. You will usually use the File Explorer for opening, accessing and rearranging folders and files in the Desktop view. You can launch the File Explorer by clicking the folder icon found on the taskbar.

The View tab in the File Explorer enables you to alter how the files appear inside the folders. For instance, you may choose to the List view when viewing documents and the Large Icons view when looking at photos. You can change the content view by selecting the View tab and then choosing your preferred view from the Layout group.

For certain folders, you can also sort your files in different ways – by name, size, file type, date modified, date created, among others. You can sort your files by selecting the View tab, clicking on the Sort by button and then choosing your preferred view from the drop-down list.

How to Search Using the File Explorer

Aside from using the Charms bar to look for files, you can also use the Search bar in the File Explorer. Actually, the File Explorer provides search options that are more advanced than those offered by the Charms bar. This is very useful when you are finding it quite hard to look for a particular document.

Every time you key in a word into the search bar, you will see that the Search Tools tab automatically opens on the Ribbon. You can find the advanced search options on the Search Tools tab. You can use them to filter your search by size, file type or date modified. You can also see the latest searches that you have made.

How to Work with Libraries

Windows 8 has 4 main libraries: Documents, Music, Pictures and Videos. Whenever you need a specific file, you can search for them through the Libraries or groups of content that you can readily access via the File Explorer.

The folders and files that you create are not actually stored in the Libraries themselves. The libraries are just there to help you better organize your stuff. You can place your own folders inside the libraries without the need to change their actual location in your computer. For instance, you can place a folder your recent photos in the Pictures library and still keep the folder on your Desktop for ready access.

Libraries are particularly vital in Windows 8 since a lot of the applications on the Start screen such as Photos, Music and Vides use the libraries in looking for and displaying their content. For instance, all of the photos in your Pictures library are also in your Photos app.

You need to note that the applications on your Start screen are optimized for media so that it will be more trouble-free for you to watch videos, listen to music and view your pictures. The File Explorer is an essential tool in organizing your current media files into libraries so that you can easily enjoy them right from your Start screen.

The My Music, My Documents folders and other certain folders are automatically included in their own applicable libraries. But you can add your own folders to any of the Libraries by first locating the Folder you want to add and then right-clicking on it. Choose the Include in library and then choose your preferred library. This technique allows your folder to be both in your library and in its original location.

Chapter 5: How to Get Started with the Desktop

The Start screen really is a cool new feature of Windows 8. But if you will be doing more than surfing the internet, watching videos and listening to music, you need to familiarize yourself with the different features in the Desktop view.

How to Work with Files

The details of the File Explorer were already discussed in the previous chapter. In this chapter, you will learn how to open and delete files, navigate through the various folders, and more.

After you have opened the File Explorer and you instantly see the document that you wish to open, you can simply double-click on it to open it. But if you still need to go through the different folders, the Navigation pane is very useful in choosing a different folder or location.

How to Delete Files

You can delete a file by clicking, holding and dragging the file directly to the Recycle Bin icon found on the Desktop. An easier way is choosing the file that you want to delete and then pressing the Delete key. Do not worry if you have unintentionally deleted a file. You can access the Recycle Bin to locate the deleted file and restore it to its original folder. You can do this by right-clicking the file that you want to restore and then choosing Restore.

But if you are certain that all files in the Recycle Bin can be permanently deleted, you can clear it by right-clicking the Recycle Bin icon and then choosing Empty Recycle bin.

How to Open an Application on the Desktop

You can do this by either clicking the application icon found on the taskbar or double-clicking the application shortcut found on the Desktop.

How to Pin Applications to the Taskbar

By default, only selected application icons will be included on your taskbar. But you can pin your most used application on the taskbar so you can readily access them. You can do this by right-clicking anyplace on the Start screen. You will then see a menu at the bottom of your screen. Choose the All apps button to show the list of all your installed applications. Look for the application you want to pin and the right-click it and then choose Pin to taskbar. You need to note, though, that you cannot pin all applications to your taskbar. There are certain applications that are designed to be launched from the Start screen only like Calendar and Messaging. Thus, you can only pin them to the Start screen.

How to Use Desktop Effects

Multi-tasking and working with several windows have become easier with Windows 8 because of the various Desktop effects now available to you.

- You can use the Snap effect to quickly resize open windows. This is particularly useful when you are working with several windows simultaneously. You can use the Snap effect by clicking, holding and dragging a window to the right or the left until you see the cursor reach the edge of your screen. Release your mouse to snap the window into place. You can easily unsnap a window by clicking, dragging it down and then releasing your mouse.

- Use the Peek effect for viewing the open windows from your taskbar. You can do this by hovering your mouse over any app icon on the taskbar that you want to view. You will then see a thumbnail preview of all open windows. You can view the full-sized window of the application by hovering the mouse over the app in the thumbnail preview.

- Use the Shake feature for selecting a single window from a clutter of open windows and then minimizing the rest. You can do this by locating and selecting the window that you want to concentrate on. You can then gently shake the window back and forth to minimize the other open windows. When you shake the window once more, all of the windows that you minimized will get maximized again.

- The Flip feature is useful in scrolling across a preview of all your open windows. You can also view any of the open applications on your Start screen using the Flip preview. The first three features – Snap, Shake and Peek – are for use only on the Desktop view. The Flip feature, on the other hand, can be used similarly in both the Desktop view and the Start screen. You can access the Flip preview by pressing and holding the Alt key and then pressing the Tab key. While you are still pressing the Alt key, press the Tab key to continue scrolling through your open windows. When you have spotted the application or the window that you want to view, stop pressing the Alt and Tab keys to display the app or window.

Conclusion

Thank you again for purchasing this book!

I hope this book was able to help you to use the new features of Windows 8.

The next step is to start personalizing your own Windows 8 so you can get the most out of it.

Finally, if you enjoyed this book, please take the time to share your thoughts and post a review on Amazon. We do our best to reach out to readers and provide the best value we can. Your positive review will help us achieve that. It'd be greatly appreciated!

Thank you and good luck!

Book 2
HTML Professional Programming Made Easy

BY SAM KEY

Expert HTML Programming Language Success in a Day for any Computer Users

Programming Box Set #96: Windows 8 Tips for Beginners & HTML Professional Programming Made Easy

Table Of Contents

Introduction

I want to thank you and congratulate you for purchasing the book, *Professional HTML Programming Made Easy: Expert HTML Programming Language Success In A Day for any Computer User!*

This book contains proven steps and strategies on how to create a web page in just a day. And if you have a lot of time in a day, you will be able to create a decent and informative website in two or three days.

HTML programming or development lessons are sometimes used as an introductory resource to programming and is a prerequisite to learning web development. In this book, you will be taught of the fundamentals of HTML. Mastering the contents of this book will make web development easier for you and will allow you to grasp some of the basics of computer programming.

To get ready for this book, you will need a desktop or laptop. That is all. You do not need to buy any expensive HTML or website development programs. And you do not need to rent a server or subscribe to a web hosting service. If you have questions about those statements, the answers are in the book.

Thanks again for purchasing this book. I hope you enjoy it!

Chapter 1: Getting Started with HTML

This book will assume that you have no prior knowledge on HTML. Do not skip reading any chapters or this book if you plan to learn about CSS, JavaScript, or any other languages that is related to web development.

HTML is a markup language. HTML defines what will be displayed on your browser and how it will be displayed. To program or code HTML, all you need is a text editor. If your computer is running on a Windows operating system, you can use Notepad to create or edit HTML files. Alternatively, if your computer is a Mac, you can use TextEdit instead.

Why is this book telling you to use basic text editors? Why are expert web developers using HTML creation programs such as Adobe Dreamweaver to create their pages? Those programs are supposed to make HTML coding easier, right?

You do not need them yet. Using one will only confuse you, especially if you do not know the fundamentals of HTML. Aside from that, web designing programs such as Adobe Dreamweaver are not all about dragging and dropping items on a web page. You will also need to be capable of manually writing the HTML code that you want on your page. That is why those programs have different views like Design and Code views. And most of them time, advanced developers stay and work more using the Code view, which is similar to a typical text editing program.

During your time learning HTML using this book, create a folder named HTML on your desktop. As you progress, you will see snippets of HTML code written here. You can try them out using your text editor and browser. You can save them as HTML files, place them into the HTML folder, and open them on your browser to see what those snippets of codes will do.

Your First HTML Page

Open your text editor and type the following in it:

Hello World!
After writing that line on your text editor, save it. On the save file dialog box, change the name of the file as firstexample.html. Do not forget the .html part. That part will serve as your file's file extension. It denotes that the file that you have saved is an HTML file and can be opened by the web browsers you have in your computer. Make sure that your program was able to save it as an .html file. Some text editor programs might still automatically add another file extension on your file name, so if that happens, you will not be open that file in your browser normally.

By the way, you do not need to upload your HTML file on a website or on the internet to view it. As long as your computer can access it, you can open it. And since your first HTML page will be in your computer, you can open it with your browser. After all, a web site can be viewed as a folder on the internet that contains HTML files that you can open.

When saving the file, make sure that it is being saved as plain text and not rich or formatted text. By default, programs such as Microsoft Word or WordPad save text files as formatted. If you saved the file as formatted, your browser might display the HTML code you have written incorrectly.

To open that file, you can try one of the three common ways. The first method is to double click or open the file normally. If you were able to save the file with the correct file extension, your computer will automatically open a browser to access the file.

The second method is to use the context menu (if you are using Windows). Right click on the file, and hover on the open with option. The menu will expand, and the list of programs that can open an HTML file will be displayed to you. Click on the browser that you want to use to open the file.

The third method is to open your browser. After that, type the local file address of your file. If you are using Windows 7 and you saved the file on the HTML folder in your desktop, then you can just type in C:\Users\User\Desktop\HTML\firstexample.html. The folder User may change depending on the account name you are using on your computer to login.

Once you have opened the file, it will show you the text you have written on it. Congratulations, you have already created a web page. You can just type paragraphs of text in the file, and it will be displayed by your browsers without problem. It is not the fanciest method, but it is the start of your journey to learn HTML.

You might be wondering, is it that easy? To be honest, yes. Were you expecting complex codes? Well, that will be tackled on the next chapter. And just to give you a heads up, it will not be complex.

This chapter has just given you an idea what is an HTML file and how you create, edit, and open one in your computer. The next chapter will discuss about tags, attributes, and elements.

Chapter 2: Elements, Properties, Tags, and Attributes

Of course, you might be already thinking: "Web pages do not contain text only, right?" Yes, you are right. In this part of the book, you will have a basic idea about how HTML code works, and how you can place some links on your page.

A web page is composed of elements. A picture on a website's gallery is an element. A paragraph on a website's article is also an element. A hyperlink that directs to another page is an element, too. But how can you do that with text alone? If you can create a web page by just using a text editor, how can you insert images on it?

Using Tags

Well, you can do that by using tags and attributes. By placing tags on the start and end of a text, you will be able to indicate what element it is. It might sound confusing, so below is an example for you to visualize and understand it better and faster:

<p>This is a paragraph that is enclosed on a paragraph tag. This is another sentence. And another sentence.</p>
In the example, the paragraph is enclosed with <p> and </p>. Those two are called HTML tags. If you enclose a block of text inside those two, the browser will understand that the block of text is a paragraph element.

Before you go in further about other HTML tags, take note that there is syntax to follow when enclosing text inside HTML tags. First, an HTML tag has two parts. The first part is the opening or starting tag. And the second part is the closing or ending tag.

The opening tag is enclosed on angled brackets or chevrons (the ones that you use to denote inequality – less and greater than signs). The closing tag, on the other hand, is also enclosed on angled brackets, but it includes a forward slash before the tag itself. The forward slash denotes that the tag is an ending tag.

Those two tags must come in pairs when you use them. However, there are HTML tags that do not require them. And they are called null or void tags. This will be discussed in another lesson. For now, stick on learning the usual HTML tags which require both opening and closing tags.

Attributes

When it comes to inserting images and links in your HTML file, you will need to use attributes. Elements have properties. The properties of each element may vary. For example, paragraph elements do not have the HREF property that anchor elements have (the HREF property and anchor element will be discussed shortly).

To change or edit those properties, you need to assign values using attributes tags. Remember, to indicate an element, use tags; to change values of the properties of elements, use attributes. However, the meanings and relations of those terms might change once you get past HTML and start learning doing CSS and JavaScript. Nevertheless, hold on to that basic idea first until you get further in web development.

Anyway, you will not actually use attributes, but you will need to indicate or assign values on them. Below is an example on how to insert a link on your web page that you will require you to assign a value on an attribute:

<a href=”www.google.com” >Google</a>
If ever you copied that, pasted or written it on your HTML file, and open your file on a browser, you will see this:

Google

In the example above, the anchor or <a> HTML tag is used. Use the anchor tag when you want to embed a hyperlink or link in your page. Any text between the opening and closing tags of the anchor tag will become the text that will appear as thc hyperlink. In the example, it is the word Google that is place between the tags and has appeared on the browser as the link.

You might have noticed the href="www.google.com" part. That part of the line determines on what page your link will direct to when you click it. That part is an example of attribute value assignment. HREF or hypertext reference is an attribute of the anchor tag.

By default, the anchor tag's value is "" or blank. In case that you do not assign any value to that attribute when you use the anchor tag, the anchor element will not become a hyperlink. Try copying and saving this line on your HTML file.

<a>Google</a>
When you open or refresh your HTML file, it will only show the word Google. It will not be underlined or will have a font color of blue. It will be just a regular text. If you hover on it, your mouse pointer will not change into the hand icon; if you click it, your browser will not do anything because the HREF value is blank.

By the way, when you assign a value on an element's or tag's attribute, you must follow proper syntax. The attribute value assignment must be inside the opening tag's chevrons and must be after the text inside the tag.

The attribute assignment must be separated from the tag with a space or spaces. The attribute's name must be type first. It must be followed by an equals sign. Then the value you want to assign to the attribute must follow the equals sign, and must be enclosed with double quotes or single quotes.

Take note, even if the number of spaces between the opening tag and the attribute assignment does not matter much, it is best that you only use one spaces for the sake of readability.

Also, you can place a space between the attribute name and the equals sign or a space between the equals sign and the value that you want to assign to the attribute. However, it is best to adhere to standard practice by not placing a space between them.

When it comes to the value that you want to assign, you can either enclosed them in double or single quotes, but you should never enclose them on a single quote and a double quote or vice versa. If you start with a single quote, end with a single quote, too. Using different quotes will bring problems to your code that will affect the way your browser will display your HTML file.

Nesting HTML Tags

What if you want to insert a link inside your paragraph? How can you do that? Well, in HTML, you can place or nest tags inside tags. Below is an example:

<p>This is a paragraph. If you want to go to Google, click this <a href="www.google.com" >link</a>.</p>
If you save that on your HTML file and open your file in your browser, it will appear like this:

This is a paragraph. If you want to go to Google, click this link.

When coding HTML, you will be nesting a lot of elements. Always remember that when nesting tags, never forget the location of the start and closing tags. Make sure that you always close the tags you insert inside a tag before closing the tag you are placing a tag inside on. If you get them mixed up, problems in your page's display will occur. Those tips might sound confusing, so below is an example of a mixed up tag:

<p>This is a paragraph. If you want to go to Google, click this <a href="www.google.com" >link</p>. And this is an example of tags getting mixed up and closed improperly.</a>

In the example, the closing tag for the paragraph tag came first before the closing tag of the anchor tag. If you copied, saved, and opened that, this is what you will get:

This is a paragraph. If you want to go to Google, click this link

. And this is an example of tag that was mixed up and closed improperly.

Since paragraphs are block elements (elements that will be always displayed on the next line and any element after them will be displayed on the next line), the last sentence was shifted to the next line. That is because the code has terminated the paragraph tag immediately.

Also, the anchor tag was closed on the end of the paragraph. Because of that, the word link up to the last word of the last sentence became a hyperlink. You should prevent that kind of mistakes, especially if you are going to code a huge HTML file and are using other complex tags that require a lot of nesting such as table tags. In addition, always be wary of the number of starting and ending tags you use. Missing tags or excess tags can also ruin your web page and fixing and looking for them is a pain.

This chapter has taught you the basic ideas about elements, properties, tags, and attributes. In coding HTML, you will be mostly fiddling around with them. In the next chapter, you will learn how to code a proper HTML document.

Chapter 3: The Standard Structure of HTML

As of now, all you can do are single lines on your HTML file. Though, you might have already tried making a page full of paragraphs and links – thanks to your new found knowledge about HTML tags and attributes. And you might be already hungry to learn more tags that you can use and attributes that you can assign values with.

However, before you tackle those tags and attributes, you should learn about the basic structure of an HTML document. The HTML file you have created is not following the standards of HTML. Even though it does work on your browser, it is not proper to just place random HTML tags on your web page on random places.

In this chapter, you will learn about the html, head, and body tags. And below is the standard structure of an HTML page where those three tags are used:

```
<!DOCTYPE html>
<html>
<head></head>
<body></body>
</html>
```

The Body and the Head

You can split an HTML document in two. The first part is composed of the things that the browser displays on your screen. And the second part is composed of the things that you will not see but is important to your document.

Call the first part as your HTML page's body. And call the second part as your HTML page's head. Every web page that you can see on the net are composed of these two parts. The tags that you have learned in the previous chapter are part of your HTML's body.

As you can see on the example, the head and body tag are nested inside the html tag. The head goes in first, while the body is the last one to appear. The order of the two is essential to your web page.

When coding in HTML, you should always place or nest all the tags or elements that your visitors will see on your HTML's body tag. On the other hand, any script or JavaScript code and styling line or CSS line that your visitors will not see must go into the head tag.

Scripts and styling lines must be read first by your browser. Even before the browser displays all the elements in your body tag, it must be already stylized and the scripts should be ready. And that is why the head tag goes first before the body.

If you place the styling lines on the end of the page, the browser may behave differently. For example, if the styling lines are placed at the end, the browser will display the elements on the screen first, and then once it reads the styling lines, the appearance of the page will change. On the other hand, if a button on your page gets clicked before the scripts for it was loaded because the scripts are placed on the end of the document, the browser will return an error.

Browsers and Checking the Source Code

Fortunately, if you forget to place the html, head, and body tags, modern browsers will automatically generate them for you. For example, try opening the HTML file that you created without the three tags with Google Chrome.

Once you open your file, press the F12 key to activate the developer console. As you can see, the html, head, and body tags were already generated for you in order to display your HTML file properly.

By the way, checking source codes is an important method that you should always use if you want to learn or imitate a website's HTML code. You can easily do it by using the developer console on Chrome or by using the context menu on other browsers and clicking on the View Page Source or View Source option.

Document Type Declaration

HTML has undergone multiple versions. As of now, the latest version is HTML5. With each version, some tags are introduced while some are deprecated. And some versions come with specifications that make them behave differently from each other. Because of that, HTML documents must include a document type declaration to make sure that your markup will be displayed just the way you wanted them to appear on your visitors' screens.

However, you do not need to worry about this a lot since it will certainly stick with HTML5, which will not be discussed in full in this book. In HTML5, document type declaration is useless, but is required. To satisfy this, all you need to do is place this on the beginning of your HTML files:

```
<!DOCTYPE html>
```

With all of those laid out, you can now create proper HTML documents. In the following chapters, the book will focus on providing you the tags that you will use the most while web developing.

Chapter 4: More HTML Tags

Now, it is time to make your HTML file to appear like a typical web page on the internet. And you can do that by learning the tags and attributes that are used in websites you stumble upon while you surf the web.

The Title Tag

First of all, you should give your web page a title. You can do that by using the <title> tag. The title of the page can be seen on the title bar and tab on your browser. If you bookmark your page, it will become the name of the bookmark. Also, it will appear on your taskbar if the page is active.

When using the title tag, place it inside the head tag. Below is an example:

```
<head>
	<title>This Is My New Web Page</title>
</head>
```

The Header Tags

If you want to organize the hierarchy of your titles and text on your web page's article, then you can take advantage of the header tags. If you place a line of text inside header tags, its formatting will change. Its font size will become bigger and its font weight (thickness) will become heavier. For example:

```
<h1> This Is the Title of This Article</h1>
<p>This is the introductory paragraph. This is another sentence. And this is the last sentence.</p>
```

If you try this example, this is what you will get:

This Is the Title of This Article

This is the introductory paragraph. This is another sentence. And this is the last sentence.

There are six levels of heading tags and they are: <h1>,<h2>,<h3>,<h4>,<h5>, and <h6>. Each level has different formatting. And as the level gets higher, the lesser formatting will be applied.

The Image Tag

First, start with pictures. You can insert pictures in your web page by using the <img> tag. By the way, the <img> tag is one of HTML tags that do not need closing tags, which are called null or empty tags. And for you to see how it works, check the example below:

```
<img
src="http://upload.wikimedia.org/wikipedia/commons/thumb/8/80
/Wikipedia-logo-v2.svg/150px-Wikipedia-logo-v2.svg.png" >
```

If you try that code and opened your HTML file, the Wikipedia logo will appear. As you can see, the <img> tag did not need a closing tag to work. As long as you place a valid value on its src (source) attribute, then an image will appear on your page. In case an image file is not present on the URL you placed on the source attribute, then a broken image picture will appear instead.

Image Format Tips

By the way, the <img> tag can display pictures with the following file types: PNG, JPEG or JPG, and GIF. Each image type has characteristics that you can take advantage of. If you are going to post photographs, it is best to convert them to JPG file format. The JPG offers decent file compression that can reduce the size of your photographs without losing too much quality.

If you need lossless quality or if you want to display a photo or image as is, then you should use PNG. The biggest drawback on PNG is that old browsers cannot read PNG images. But that is almost a thing of a past since only handful people use old versions of browsers.

On the other hand, if you want animated images on your site, then use GIFs. However, take note that the quality of GIF is not that high. The number of colors it can display is few unlike PNG and JPG. But because of that, its size is comparatively smaller than the two formats, which is why some web developers convert their sites' logos as GIF to conserve space and reduce loading time.

The Ordered and Unordered List

Surely, you will place lists on your web pages sooner or later. In HTML, you can create two types of lists: ordered and unordered. Ordered lists generate alphanumeric characters to denote sequence on your list while unordered lists generate symbols that only change depending on the list level.

To create ordered lists, use the <ol> and <li> tag. The <ol> tag defines that the list will be an ordered one, and the <li> or list item tag defines that its content is considered a list item on the list. Below is an example:

```
<h1>Animals</h1>
<ol>
	<li>dog</li>
	<li>cat</li>
	<li>mouse</li>
</ol>
```

This will be the result of that example:

Animals

1. dog
2. cat
3. mouse

On the other hand, if you want an unordered list, you will need to use the <ul> tag. Like the <ol> tag, you will still need to use the <li> tag to denote the list items. Below is an example:

```
<h1>Verbs</h1>
<ul>
	<li>walk</li>
	<li>jog</li>
	<li>run</li>
</ul>
```

This will be the result of that example:

Verbs

- walk
- jog
- run

Instead of numbers, the list used bullets instead. If ever you use the <li> tag without <ol> or <ul>, browsers will usually create them as unordered lists.

Nesting Lists

You can nest lists in HTML to display child lists. If you do that, the browser will accommodate it and apply the necessary tabs for the child list items. If you nest unordered lists, the bullets will be changed to fit the child list items. Below is an example:

```
<h1>Daily Schedule</h1>
<ul>
	<li>Morning</li>

	<ul>
		<li>Jog</li>
		<li>Shower</li>
		<li>Breakfast</li>
	</ul>
	<li>Afternoon</li>
	<ul>
		<li>Lunch</li>
		<li>Watch TV</li>
```

```
    </ul>
    <li>Evening</li>
    <ul>
        <li>Dinner</li>
        <li>Sleep</li>
    </ul>
</ul>
```

This will be the result of that example:

Daily Schedule

- Morning
  - Jog
  - Shower
  - Breakfast
- Afternoon
  - Lunch
  - Watch TV
- Evening
  - Dinner
  - Sleep

And with that, you should be ready to create a decent website of your own. But for now, practice using those tags. And experiment with them.

Conclusion

Thank you again for purchasing this book!

I hope this book was able to help you to become knowledgeable when it comes to HTML development. With the fundamentals you have learned, you can easily explore the vast and enjoyable world of web development. And that is no exaggeration.

The next step is to learn more tags and check out websites' sources. Also, look for HTML development tips. Then learn more about HTML5 and schema markup. Those things will help you create richer web sites that are semantically optimized.

On the other hand, if you want to make your website to look cool, then you can jump straight to leaning CSS or Cascading Style Sheets. Cascading Style Sheets will allow you to define the appearance of all or each element in your web page. You can change font size, weight, color, and family of all the text on your page in a whim. You can even create simple animations that can make your website look modern and fancy.

If you want your website to be interactive, then you can start learning client side scripting with JavaScript or Jscript too. Scripts will provide your web pages with functions that can make it more alive. An example of a script function is when you press a button on your page, a small window will popup.

Once you master all of that, then it will be the best time for you to start learning server side scripting such as PHP or ASP. With server side scripting, you can almost perform everything on websites. You can take information from forms and save them to your database. Heck, you can even create dynamic web pages. Or even add chat functions on your website.

Finally, if you enjoyed this book, please take the time to share your thoughts and post a review on Amazon. We do our best to reach out to readers and provide the best value we can. Your positive review will help us achieve that. It'd be greatly appreciated!

Thank you and good luck!

Check Out My Other Books

Below you'll find some of my other popular books that are popular on Amazon and Kindle as well. Simply click on the links below to check them out. Alternatively, you can visit my author page on Amazon to see other work done by me.

C Programming Success in a Day

Android Programming in a Day

C Programming Professional Made Easy

C ++ Programming Success in a Day

Python Programming in a Day

PHP Programming Professional Made Easy

JavaScript Programming Made Easy

CSS Programming Professional Made Easy

Windows 8 Tips for Beginners

Programming Box Set #96: Windows 8 Tips for Beginners & HTML Professional Programming Made Easy

If the links do not work, for whatever reason, you can simply search for these titles on the Amazon website to find them.

www.ingramcontent.com/pod-product-compliance
Lightning Source LLC
Chambersburg PA
CBHW060931050326
40689CB00013B/3052
* 9 7 8 1 5 1 8 7 3 7 4 3 5 *